This edition copyright © 2002 Lion Publishing

Published by
**Lion Publishing plc**
Mayfield House, 256 Banbury Road,
Oxford OX2 7DH, England
www.lion-publishing.co.uk
ISBN 0 7459 4801 4

First edition 2002
1 3 5 7 9 10 8 6 4 2 0

### Picture acknowledgments

Picture research by Zooid Pictures Limited.

7: André Burian/Corbis UK Ltd. 9: Philip Gould/Corbis UK Ltd.
11: Nubar Alexanian/Corbis UK Ltd. 13: Digital Art/Corbis UK Ltd.
15: Bettmann/Corbis UK Ltd. 16/17: Japack Photo Library/Corbis UK Ltd.
19: Richard Hamilton Smith/Corbis UK Ltd. 20/21: David Hanover/Corbis UK Ltd.
22: Archivo Iconografico, S.A./Corbis UK Ltd. 24/25: Anna Clopet/Corbis UK Ltd.
27: Lois Ellen Frank/Corbis UK Ltd. 29: Galen Rowell/Corbis UK Ltd.

### Text acknowledgments

6: Thomas J. Cottle. 8: John Keats. 10: Louise Bogan. 12: Martin Buber.
14: Leon Bloy. 16: Corrie ten Boom. 18: Paul Tillich. 20/21: Ursula K. Le Guin.
23: Richard Jeffries. 24: Chinese proverb. 26: William Blake. 28/29: Psalm 30:5,
taken from The New Revised Standard Version of the Bible, Anglicized Edition,
copyright © 1989, 1995 by the Division of Christian Education of the National
Council of the Churches of Christ in the United States of America, and used
by permission. All rights reserved.

A catalogue record for this book is available
from the British Library

Typeset in Novarese
Printed and bound in Singapore

# joy

in words and images

LION
Giftlines

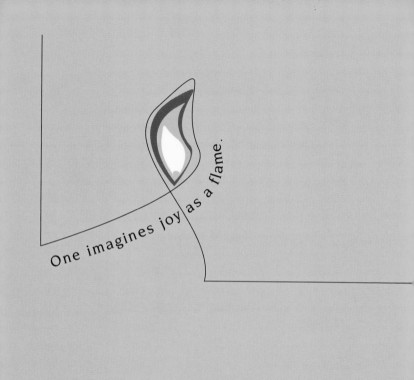

One imagines joy as a flame.

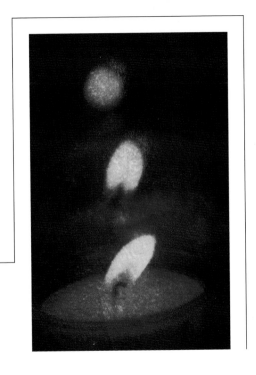

A thing of beauty
is a joy for ever:
Its loveliness
increases.

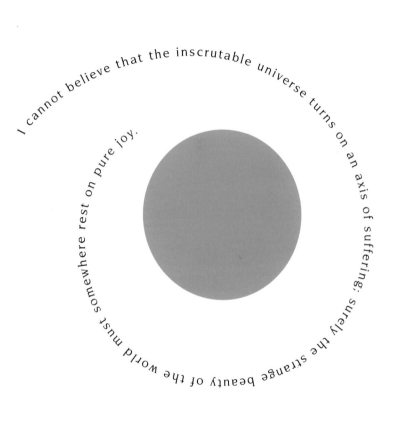

I cannot believe that the inscrutable universe turns on an axis of suffering; surely the strange beauty of the world must somewhere rest on pure joy.

The
beating
heart of the
universe
is holy
joy.

Joy is the most infallible sign
of the presence of God.

_____

Joy

runs

deeper

than

despair.

For in the depth is truth;

and in the depth is hope;

and in the depth is joy.

What I was given
was the thing
you can't earn,
and can't keep,
and often don't
even recognize
at the time;

_____ I mean joy.

It is about me

It is
eternity
now.
I am in
the midst
of it.

in the sunshine.

One joy

  s c a t t e r s

a hundred griefs.

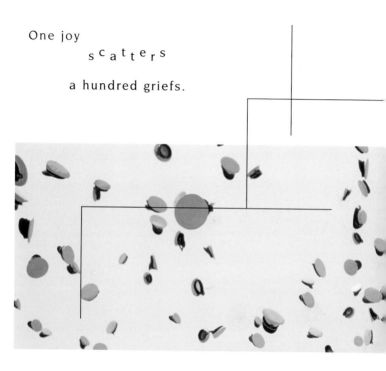

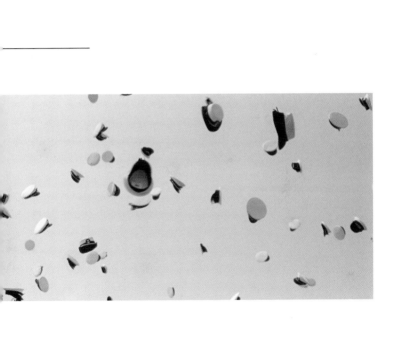

He who binds to himself a joy

Doth the winged life destroy

But he who kisses the joy as it flies ⎯⎯

Lives in Eternity's

sunrise

Weeping may linger for the night,

_____ but joy comes with the morning.